CRICKET POETRY

By

Arthur Salway

© 2013 Arthur Salway. All rights reserved.
ISBN 978-1-291-49637-6

Dedication

To my father, Reginald Arthur Salway, to whom I owe so much; not least my appreciation of the "noble game."

AUTHOR'S PREFACE

The following 47 cricket poems were written over a period of some 20 years, during and after my playing days. In 2001 fourteen were put on line and later eight more were added, juxtaposed with cricket photographs. The response from cricket lovers worldwide was, and remains, immensely gratifying and has provided the encouragement I needed to publish the book in your hands.
May I express my thanks to my former team mate Keith Westell for his initial persuasion to go on line, and to his "Webmaster" son Jari, whose help in producing "Cricket Poetry" has been invaluable. I hope you enjoy my poems.

Arthur Salway

Photographs by kind permission of West Hill Park School, Titchfield, Hampshire.

CONTENTS

Hampshire Secret 7
A turn of the wrist 8
Alive And Well 10
Appearances 13
C.B.Final 2012 14
Captain Grumpy 16
Cricket Teas 17
Facing Facts 18
Fast Spin 19
Golden Moment 22
Indian Takeaway 23
It's Just Not Cricket 24
Legacies - India 2008 25
Over 28
Pavilion in Winter 30
Prodigy 32
Reflections 33
Revisited 34
Sackcloth and Ashes 35
Scorebook 36
Side-on 38
Straight Blade 39
Team Kit Bag 40
The Amateurs 42
The Cameo 43
The Commentators 44

The Cricket Field 46

The Cricket Widow 47

The English Game 49

The First Ball 50

The Nightwatchman 50

The Old Ball 50

The Pavilion End 50

The Skipper 50

The Toss 50

Tragedy at St. Helen's 50

Umpiring 50

What's in a Name 50

Why? 50

Hampshire Secret

The Solent; where the Itchen and the Test
Refresh the swirling seas from East and West;
Where liners plough their furrows to the sun,
And trawlers toil while yachtsmen have their fun.
There lies, submerged, the Brambles sandbank, which is
One of Hampshire's least known cricket pitches.

Least known, least used, for reason plain to see.
Only in England could such madness be!
Just once or twice a year in this wild place
The tide-scoured Brambles bares its rheumy face
In daylight hours and weather of the sort
Required by cricketers to take their sport.

No grass is here, no boundaries or hedges;
Just boats and dinghies drawn up round its edges.
A massive tide – an hour, or maybe more
Before the players must head back to the shore
Time for a sandwich? Perhaps a flask of tea,
A wary eye on the approaching sea.

And so, at "maximum-low-water-spring"
A mariner may witness this strange thing;
A cricket match surrounded by the ocean.
Who shall believe him? Such a foolish notion!
A sight that makes him rub his wondering eyes
That none but the English could, or would, devise.

Ten overs each. The players on the Brambles
Enjoy what is a quite delightful shambles.
Waves and cheers from passing English yachtsmen,
And something incoherent from a Scotsman!
Their fixture list is empty as it stands.
Perhaps T/20 on the Goodwin Sands?

Can we understand them? Yes, we can.
Cricket feeds the boy within a man.
Something in such foolishness is bright;
And not a risk assessment form in sight.
The future's not as bleak as it may seem
While Brambles bank still hosts its cricket team.

A turn of the wrist

Soccer is won with cultured feet
And rugger with grit and grist;
But when cricket is played the difference is made
By a delicate turn of the wrist.

Our modern-day players are athletes
But expertise doesn't consist
Of power or pace: take W. G. Grace,
It was all in his turn of the wrist.

Give K.P. a well pitched up straight one
That would bowl any batsman who missed,
And it's off middle peg and down through long leg
With a powerful turn of the wrist.

When Warne thinks a batsman can read him
He'll bowl one he cannot resist.
It isn't the grunt that gets him up front
It's the well-disguised turn of the wrist.

It helps if a chap's double jointed
As slow motion replays will tell.
In the instance of Murali, I fancy there's surely
A turn of the elbow as well.

It's not only batsmen and bowlers
From artistry will not desist;
"Owzat?" they all shout, and the mans given out
With an elegant turn of the wrist.

So never mind muscles and fitness
And everything else on the list;
When alls said and done, this game can be won
By no more than a turn of the wrist.

A Winter's Tale

Winter; loads of jobs to do.
They can wait an hour or two.
Get my feet up, can't be bad;
Cricket's on from Trinidad.

A cricket lover's heart rejoices
To hear those old familiar voices;
Imagining the field of play
Courtesy of C.M.J.

Blower's voice drones on and on.
"Oops! Another wicket gone!"
Luminaries then explain
Why Pietersen has failed again.

Gents with headphones in the street,
Brollies, bowlers, all complete.
Passers-by would never guess
They're listening to T.M.S.

Old opponents chipping in,
Antagonisms wearing thin,
Add impartial interjections
To Agger's jolly recollections.

"Thirty in the shade" sounds right:
Same as here in Fahrenheit.
Half past four and getting dark.
Lunchtime at Sabina Park.

"Noises off" are disconcerting.
Enough to start your eardrums hurting.
Conche shells blow and steel bands play,
Like Headingly on Roses' day!

Five short days consume the game:
Longwave/FM both the same.
Join you on the air again
Next week-end from Port of Spain.

Alive And Well

Stapleton in June. The sun shines down
Upon the cricket ground beside the town.
Spectators congregate and very soon
Forget their troubles for the afternoon,
Relishing an English summer's bliss.
Through bitter winter months they longed for this.

The visitors from Frome have won the toss
And batting first, are 30 without loss.
Visiting players, age obscure,
Having played here many times before,
Begin to wander by the dry stone walls
Responding to raised hands and welcome calls,
Greeting the spectators, some by name,
(Would this take place with any other game?)
And sitting with them, settle at their ease
Beside the walls and underneath the trees,
Then slowly, very slowly, working round
Renew old friendships all around the ground;
Men of different status, age, and kind
Seeking and finding those of kindred mind,
Impartial as they venture and compare
Opinions of proceedings on the square.

Discussing prospects, memories, the wicket:
What do they have in common? Only cricket.
In other circles they would never meet
Or, silent, pass each other in the street.
As wickets fall spectators must release
Protagonist companions to the crease
Their conversations promised to resume
When next the first team plays at home to Frome.

"Ref assaulted", "Jostling at Lords",
"Team bus stoned" in pictures and in words
The press and media never fail to mention
The foul language, violence and tension
So prevalent in sport and, so it seems,
Between supporters of opposing teams.
The cameras and press we may assume
Will not be there when Stapleton play Frome

NB. The related events at Stapleton were witnessed when revisiting the ground In 1992.

An Odd Bunch

Games of cricket, crookedness apart,
Have carried wagers from the very start.
"Not at Brookfield School," I hear you mutter;
But should you ever contemplate a flutter,
Setting odds may prove a trifle hard.
So, if we did, then this might be the card.

It's 3 to 1 we'll all turn out in white
And "evens" that we're rained off on the night.
Twenty runs for Lambo's worth a shout,
And 2 to 1 that Eddy runs him out.
50 to 1 a bowler gets a hat-trick,
And "evens" on a golden duck for Patrick.

3 to 1 that Brookfield win the match,
And 2 to 1 that Cowlly drops a catch.
10 to 1 a throw-in hits the sticks
And odds declined that Robbo's hit for six.
5 to 1 that Keppler fluffs a chance
Make it a double that he splits his pants!

If you're short of cash or feeling thrifty
Take 10 to 1 on Williamson reaching fifty.
Odds on no-balls have to be denied
But 5 to 1 that Grumpy bowls a wide.
2 to 1 or "evens", there's some doubt,
That Barry Stares will swear when he is out.

It's 5 to 1 a snick goes undetected,
And 6 to 1 that Arty gets selected.
These are the latest odds we can provide
And they can change as quickly as the side.
But "Mums the Word," the last time OFSTED missed 'em.
The I.P.L.'s got nothing on our system!

When the match is over and you don't know where we are
The odds on our location is -- 10 to 1 bar!

P.S. Copyright waived on this one. Try putting your own team names in

Anticipation

I seem to have more energy than usual today;
There's a jauntiness about me that just won't go away.
No matter that the car won't start or that the boiler's failed
I'm feeling optimistic, bright eyed and bushy tailed.

The clocks went "on" last Sunday, the daffodils are out.
That helps to cheer a fellow up but nonetheless I doubt
If that's what makes me chipper. I think I know the reason.
I guarantee it's down to the approaching cricket season.

Actually it's started, but neither you nor I
Can take much interest in a match they're playing in Dubai.
Real cricket's played much nearer home, or so it would appear.
If you're like me you'd rather see things happening back here.

Like mowers on the outfield, rollers on the square;
Chaps with brushes in their hands painting here and there.
"Nets" in local sports halls to get us in the mood;
Never mind the temperature, life is looking good.

I'd better find my cricket bag and sort out all my gear;
So much to do, so little time, the season's nearly here.
Wash and press my cricket flannels, get the grass stains out;
Will they fit? I must admit, there really is some doubt.

For you and I, in days gone by, preparatory toil
Would have us grubbing 'round in tool sheds finding linseed oil
To sharpen up our trusty blades, (Oh, that lovely smell),
Then slapping loads of blanco on our buckskin boots as well.

While progress has deprived us of such delightful measures
Anticipation stands supreme among our earthly pleasures.
Nothing ever spoils it, so never under-rate it.
Cricket's coming back again so let's anticipate it.

Appearances

Take Tom, for instance, in the slips,
Arms akimbo, hands on hips,
Creamy whites & old club sweater,
A chap could hardly turn out better.
His cap in burgundy & yellow
Gives some kudos to the fellow;
He dropped the opener at the start,
So what? At least he looked the part.
The skipper wishes all his men did
Manage to appear so splendid.

A cricketer, it must be said,
Should have a cap upon his head
Consistent with the fading dream
In caramel & mauve & cream,
Conjuring images of Eton,
Of carrying one's bat, unbeaten;
Rich & famous flannelled fools,
Amateurs from Public Schools,
Trevor Bailey, Norman Yardley,
Freddie Truman? no, well hardly!

The modern cap has no panache
Its baseball stylo is cheap & brash
They make us old boys rage & tremble
Convinced that cricketers resemble
Norman Wisdom or Jack Horner
Selling peanuts on the corner;
No hoops, no segments, stripes or rings,
No funny little button things;
How can a chappie be admired
When so stupidly attired?

Those buckskin boots are father fine, Circa 1949.
Ankle deep in eyelet holes
Bash-in studs and leather soles,
Just the job for kicking doors,
Roughing up pavilion floors
And, in the twilight years of cricket,
Stopping boundaries, at mid-wicket;
Substantial, so you'd never know
You'd stopped a yorker on the toe.

It's sometimes rather hard I fear
To lay your hands on classy gear,
Flannels flatter any bloke
So get 'em made in cream, bespoke.
Never mind if standards lapse
Join the clubs with decent caps,
And finally, if all else fails,
Visit local jumble sales
Rummage round & if your luck's in
You might find some boots- in buckskin!

So cheer up sir – don't be dejected,
Look the part & get selected.

C.B.Final 2012

Lords; headquarters of the game and home of its tradition
And venue for the final of the Clydesdale competition.
Happy to be underdogs, the "Hampshire Royals" are here
To play the county champions, the "Bears" from Warwickshire.
The ambience is quite superb. Who could ask for more,
Or who anticipate the pleasure that we have in store?

How apt that Hampshire should be here. It was, as I recall,
On Hambledon's Broadhalfpenny Down beside "The Bat and Ball"
That cricket shed its adolescence. As for Thomas Lord,
He's buried at West Meon underneath the churchyard sward;
And Warwickshire, the home of Shakespeare; what more can we say?
The atmospheric scene is set. Nostalgia rules O.K.?

Put in to bat, no harm in that, our lads prove more than ready.
They all chip in, we just might win if we can take things steady.
Two-four-five at six-point-one the total to defend.
The "Royals" will make a fight of it, on that you may depend.
No Danny Briggs or Mascarenhas in the side today;
"Cometh the hour – cometh the man" is what the old boys say.

Ian Bell is going well but Woody's bowling corkers
And Kabby kills the power-play with toe-nail-clipping yorkers.
Clarke and Woakes are useful blokes and put their side in clover.
Seven runs is all they need off one remaining over.
The tension is unbearable; as someone said this morning,
"Tickets for a Hampshire match should carry a health warning".

The bookies are on valium, the betting is on hold.
Warwickshire are odds-on favourites, so we have been told,
But Hampshire have a history of victory at the death.
Kabir Ali's running in; the Hogs all hold their breath.
One run off the first one, another off the second;
They're getting them in singles just like Maurice Leyland reckoned!

Hampshire need a wicket, or else the runs will come.
The "Bears" are looking chipper and the "Royals" are looking glum.
Then Ali castles Blackwell. What a hullabaloo;
And every pigeon Lords possesses heads for pastures new.
Nearby, at the Palace, the Queen was taking tea.
"What's that?" she cried. The Duke replied, "I think it's World War 3

Only 5 off 2 to get and Carter at the crease.
Come on Kabir, bowl a dot or else a yorker - PLEASE.
Oh no! We can't believe it. We can't take any more.
The batsman swings, the ball takes wings, and runs away for four.
This game is like a roller-coaster. It's the very devil.
It can't be true but what say you; the bloomin' scores are level.

Neck and neck. A last ball finish. There is nothing in it.
If people are engraving things they'll only have a minute.
Kabir turns. He's running in. We wonder how he feels.
Everything depends on him. He's kicking up his heels.
He goes side-on, he leaps, he bowls, the wickie takes it sweetly
And, with a cry of exultation, wrecks the stumps completely.

The Hogs erupt, they cheer, they shout; such energy's expended,
That in the "House" debating time is temporarily suspended.
And what of poor old Warwickshire? You very often find
"If only" is the thing that preys on everybody's mind.
"If only I had gone for two," "If only I'd not dropped it,"
"If only I'd not bowled that wide," "If only I had stopped it."

So back to Hampshire with the Cup; another trophy more,
And Monday morning finds the skipper at the Chairman's door.
"There is a little matter Sir I'd bring to your attention
That what with all the fussing Sir I quite forgot to mention.
For all the upgrades at the Bowl, and all the fancy stuff,
The Trophy Cabinet's no good. It isn't big enough!

Written for Hampshire C.C.C. to celebrate their successes in competitions.

Captain Grumpy

We'd travelled independently and, wonders never ceased,
We'd all got there with time to spare. The skipper would be pleased.
It gave him "options" as he said, a chance to put them in
Without the need to borrow fielders so we could begin.
Imagine our bewilderment when, taken unaware,
We heard our favourite skipper say, "I'm not a happy bear."

In fact to tell the honest truth we weren't surprised because
A "happy bear" was something that our skipper rarely was.
He'd play the devil's advocate, be miserable as sin
So he could make a fuss of us if ever we should win.
Pretending he was furious to keep us on our toes
He vented his displeasure at our choice of casual clothes.

"We're up for it today," he said, "we haven't come for fun.
They're looking at you now my boys, the contest has begun.
Do you look like cricketers? Look at those shirts; good grief.
Where did you posers think this fixture was; in Tenerife?
I don't expect a bunch of toffs with panamas and hampers
But you should see yourselves; you're like a load of washed out campers!"

"As if you scruffs weren't bad enough to give their team a break,
They'll have to smile at that great pile of kit for pity's sake.
You might roll up in B.M.W.s, Mercs and E type Jags
But only wallies put their gear in Sainsbury's plastic bags.
And where did someone get that grip? OK. I'll stick my neck out.
You nicked it off a hippy with his back turned at the check-out."

We laughed so long and heartily the skipper gave a grin.
"O.K.", he said, "I'll let you off, but get out there and win."
We all enjoyed the team-talk; it wasn't quite the norm.
With wit if not with kit we knew the skipper was on form.
The other team were watching, and worrying I'd say.
Any confidence they had our laughter took away.

Cricket Teas

Gastronomic pleasure needs an ambience to complete it.
Enjoying food is often just a case of where you eat it.
You don't need gourmet recipes it may be safely said;
Try ice-cream in the sauna or a glass of wine in bed.
And sandwiches with cucumber are guaranteed to please
When eaten in pavilions as part of cricket teas.

Is it imagination or a complex I have got,
Or does tea taste much fresher from a brown enamel pot?
Is home-made cake superior (and fruitier as well)
To the neat and tidy versions that the supermarkets sell?
Is it just my fancy or exertions at the wicket
That makes food taste much better half way through a game of cricket?

There are elbows on the tables, and fellows start with cake.
If we were boys we'd get told off for all the noise we make.
Laughter, chat, and bonhomie. "Another sausage roll sir?"
The scrape of studs on wooden boards, the chink of cup and saucer.
It's so laid back you'd never know we were in competition.
What other game includes a picnic with the opposition?

Old team photos line the walls, the setting is sublime.
The girls have turned up trumps again; they do it every time.
Lots of "naughty-no-noes" and things we shouldn't touch.
We'll struggle in the field if we give in and eat too much.
"Another sandwich gentlemen? Another cup of tea?"
The opening bowlers should decline. Thank goodness that's not me!

The captains are the first to stir, the game must be resumed.
Our cricket tea is all but done, the sandwiches consumed.
How fortunate the batting side, their openers apart;
They can let their tea go down while we, the fielders, start
To try to get their batsmen out. I shouldn't think they'd make
Much more than fifty weighted down with Andy's mother's cake!

Facing Facts

Im getting old, Im getting plump, the future's looking murky;
The only bird I'll ever pull will be the Christmas turkey!
My buckskin boots need insoles and the moths have got my flannels,
And games of cricket aren't forthcoming from the usual channels.
I wait to be selected but I wait 'til "ad finitum";
My club's defunct and half my kit is a collector's item.
My sweater doesn't fit me and my stripey cap is smelly,
And Sky T.V. has bought the rights to cricket on the telly.
Another summer's come and gone, another season past.
It seems that game three years ago was probably my last.
Just as well I didn't know, it would have spoiled my fun;
Actually I bowled quite well- took 3 for 21.
What to do with all my gear? It mocks me 'though I love it.
I'd better rack my brains to find a secret place to shove it.
My tidy wife is after if - "Get rid of it" she'll say,
"You'll never play again so why not chuck the stuff away."
She's right of course and what she says is only common sense,
But I am still a cricketer - in the present tense,
And I can still delude myself it isn't 'if but 'when'
I'll squeeze into my cricket togs and trot out once again.
But dreams are dreams and facts are facts, it's likely that I shant,
And p'raps it's better if I don't - I might find out I can't!

Fast Spin

When we were boys and striding to the wicket,
Learning life while we were playing cricket,
"The bowling good?" we'd ask as we went in;
Departing batsmen scowled & said, "Fast spin".

Two dreaded words to cause a youngster's heart
To lose all confidence before the start.
What use technique or grim determination?
Who could survive such awesome combination?

We learned that speed faced up to seems less daunting;
That spin is nothing if the length is wanting;
That some the obstacles will overstate,
While runs come gradually to those who wait.

And later, in life's seventy over match,
When adversaries threaten to dispatch
Our hopes and dreams before they can begin
Those childhood words come back to us - "Fast spin".

In 2010 Hampshire and Somerset met in the final of the T/20 competition at Southampton. The match was not decided until the last ball of the :-

Final Over

Some people play computer games with tanks and bombs and swords,
But we get our excitement at the Rose Bowl or at Lord's.
Take Saturday for instance, there were thrills and spills a-plenty
As Hampshire took on Somerset in cricket's Twenty/20.
Throughout the match each side had seen its hopes and dreams diminish
But rallied round to conjure up a quite fantastic finish,

"The outcome of a hundred matches," commentary recalls,
"Has boiled down to what will happen in the next six balls."
The ethos was electric, all eyes were on the wicket.
All over Hampshire radios were tuned in to the cricket.
Nails were bitten to the quick; no-one missed a ball.
No-one left to queue for buses - nobody at all.

Who will bowl the final over? Hampshire held its breath.
Who will Trescothick trust to bowl those yorkers at the death?
He is an old campaigner; he must know what he's doin'.
Caddick's hung his boots up so it has to be De Bruyn.
"Eight from six" is not, perhaps, as easy as it seems
With twenty-thousand-plus supporters roaring on their teams.

The first ball is a bouncer that flies past Christian's head.
To get things done they need a run so Sean's on strike instead.
If anybody's going to make it Ervine is the man
So out the way there Linford Christie, let them run as can!
The wickie misses with his throw, our hopes are still alive.
A bye it proves, the target moves to "seven runs off five."

De Bruyn charges in again; he's under stress poor chappie.
Let's hope he bowls some loose ones and makes all Hampshire happy.
The ball is good, one has to say much better than the shot.
A groan goes round the Rose Bowl and the scorer puts a dot.
The game is swinging round to favour Somerset once more;
We've only gone from "eight from six" to "seven runs from four."

The sky grows black and overcast, lowering o'er the scene.
It could presage, at this late stage, that rain may intervene.
If all else fails except the gales then what the team could do is
Pray for rain and win the game with thanks to Duckworth-Lewis!
De Bruyn bowls a short one and Ervine pulls it round;
Up into the floodlights ---- and safely to the ground.

Two runs taken; "five from three," and Ervine still on strike.
The tension is unbearable; we've never known the like.
Will De Bruyn hold one back or will he push one through?
What matters more is Hampshire's score and what Ervine can do.
Not much it seems, our little dreams are darkening with the sky.
"Four from two" it is then thanks to yet another bye.

In fact, and here's a funny thing peculiar to cricket,
Even "three from two" will do if we don't lose a wicket.
Dan Christian is the batsman now and hits the winning run –
Oh no! The fielder's saved the four. We had to say well done.
What a day and what a match; it's one almighty tussle.
Wait a minute; something's happened. Christian's pulled a muscle!

It soon became apparent that a runner was desired
So enter Jimmy Adams wearing all that was required.
The umpire asked the groundsman, "Is that the line or ain't it?
You'd better mix your white stuff up and get out here and paint it."
Everything was happening as the game went to the wire.
We wouldn't have been surprised if the pavilion caught fire!

Last ball – and still the winners are impossible to choose.
It was a game that neither side, in truth, deserved to lose.
"One from one." A win, a loss, a tie, Which shall it be?
--and done without the aid of Mascarhenas and K.P.
De Bruyn bowls an in-swinger. It's there or therabout'
It hits the pad, the crowd go mad, "Owzat?" opponents shout.

Dan Christian, immunised from pain, forgets the laws of cricket,
And, knowing that a run is on, goes charging down the wicket.
Jimmy Adans does the same, and Ervine doesn't linger
But will the cogitating umpire raise the dreaded finger?
Meanwhile the run has been completed; justice has been done.
Corky runs onto the field convinced the Royals have won.

In fact we should have lost because, though cricketers aren't fools,
Somerset could well have prospered if they'd known the rules;
And if the Rose Bowl had a roof with all a roof entails
Be sure it would have followed as the umpires raised the bails.
The Hogs all went delirious and raised a mighty cheer,
And Somerset Spudsuckers started crying in their beer.

Corky took the trophy and with joy he held it up.
Hampshire's gallant lads had won the Twenty/20 Cup.
It was so emotional it made us blub and choke,
And our late night celebrations could be heard in Basingstoke.
While others head for Taunton. Are they downhearted? No.
They love their Twenty/20 where the cider apples grow.

Golden Moment

At Brookfield one night we witnessed a sight
In the annals of cricket most rare,
The skip won the call and gave the new ball
To a bald headed opening pair.

Their batsmen looked good but try as they would
The ball wouldn't get off the square,
for such was the style, the experience and guile
Of the bald headed opening pair.

They were dazzled, confused, and completely bemused,
There was no way on earth they'd prepare
for a contest, my friends, not from one, but both ends
With a bald headed opening pair.

Their innings was done for less that a ton,
Their game plan was up in the air
We concluded, no doubt they had reckoned without
Our bald headed opening pair.

We batted great guns and knocked off the runs
With two or three overs to spare.
Magoo made a few but the victory was due
To the bald headed opening pair.

The scorebook won't show it, so no-one will know it
But the fortunate few who were there,
And its their claim to fame that they played in a game
With a bald headed opening pair.

My team mates, mine host; I give you a toast,
To captaincy extr'ordinaire,
And to Barry and Ken, those remarkable men,
The bald headed opening pair.

Indian Takeaway

What an experience! Well, well well.
Have you been watching the I.P.L.?
Fast and furious and frenetic,
Unbelievably athletic.
There goes a big one. Well hit pal.
That's on its way to the Taj Mahal.
Massive stadia old and new,
Pretty girls that dance on cue,
Happy families round the ground,
Players wired up for sound.
Crash – bang-- wallop. Did you see
That sixer? Goodness gracious me!
Nice to think our legacy
To India's new democracy
Included cricket for their leisure
And quite extr'ordinary pleasure.
Mumbai Indians are in clover;
Twenty seven off the over!
Well heeled sponsors cough up millions
To get the stars in their pavilions.
Players vie to make the teams
And wealth beyond their wildest dreams.
"Never mind the bloomin' Ashes;
Get your name down where the cash is".
Down in the bars at the M.C.C.
Over a glass of G and T,
Tongues are wagging, heads are shaking;
Is this a rod for our backs they're making?
Will players go or will they stay?
Watch out for an Indian takeaway.

It's Just Not Cricket

Cricket is a gentleman's pursuit,
Synonymous with fairness; branch and root.
Born of a time when fellows knew their place
And no-one was inclined to court disgrace.
The schoolmaster, the doctor and the squire
Received the deference dignities require.
We wonder what the players of yesteryear
Would make of all the banter that we hear.

What's happened since those balmy halcyon days
To change the state of mind in which one plays,
To loosen tongues to challenge a decision
And greet opponents efforts with derision?
A game that once united now divides
And rancour is observed between the sides.
Bowlers glare and swear and play it tough.
Skill and application aren't enough.

Wicket-keepers, far from being the joker,
Endlessly applaud the mediocre,
Suggesting that the pitch has got some fizz
And that the bowling's better than it is.
"Oh yes Arty boy! That was a good'un"
Won't turn me into Muralitheran.
Most bowlers know the way to ply their cause
Without a constant barrage of applause.

We look, in hope, to the professional game
And find the non-stop verbal's just the same;
In fact, if anything, it's even worse.
You wonder if it's something they rehearse,
Or if, perhaps, their efforts would relent
Without the tirade of encouragement.
W all have jobs to do but there's no doubt
We won't get clapped unless we get clapped-out!

Edwardians would be speechless, if you please,
To hear the booes that welcome to the crease
Opposing captains, players of repute.
Surely such boorishness deserves the boot.
Our game, once watched in quiet contemplation,
Has sought support and suffered transformation.
Cricket has a "nouveau clientele".
The Barmy Army is alive and well!

Legacies - India 2008

It's time to get the Union Jacks unfurled
And celebrate what we have given the world:
Colonial legacies, some bad, some good,
Like Marmite, Oxo, ties and Yorkshire pud,
Rugger, Weetabix and garden gnomes,
Democracy, roast beef and Sherlock Holmes.
But which has served our former colonies best?
Is there just one that stands out from the rest?

"Of course there is!" we cry without hypocrisy
And something ten times better than democracy;
Something tailor-made for sunny weather,
A game that binds its devotees together,
Regardless of their cultures and their creeds,
Their temperaments, their foibles, and their needs;
Overcoming politics and colour
And fostering respect for one another.

We Brits invented cricket to enjoy it.
Then used the British Empire to deploy it.
At first the locals really had no say in it.
At the point of Corporal Jones's bayonet
They helped clear pitches in remote locations
For ex-pat clubs, posh schools, and mission stations.
They watched, they learned, they thought they'd like to try it;
With home-made kit they practiced on the quiet.
Little did they dream as well they might.
Of the day they'd stuff the English out of sight!

But just in case our pride becomes absurd
I think the Indians ought to have a word.
There's something in our English game you see
That is distinctly Indian - it's "tea".
"Lunch" is Anglo-Saxon, so is "drinks",
But "tea" is old colonial methinks.
It's thanks to India, it seems to me,
That cricketers world-wide adjourn for "tea".

How apt that England's brave but vanquished boys
Should get the chance to experience all the joys
Of genuine cups of pukkha Indian char
While getting soundly stuffed at Chandigarh,
Then sample some Assam and maybe more,
While getting stuffed again at Ranjipoor.
And when morale is low and senses reeling
There's nothing like a throatful of Darjeeling!

On top of coming home with no rewards
They're back to squeezing tea bags down at Lords.
At least they've seen how cricket should be played
And how a proper cup of tea is made
That neutralises juices in the belly.
(They don't get indigestion back in Delhi)
And when their team takes "tea" they will remember
The way the Indians stuffed them last December!

Off Breaks

Matches usually begin
With sweaty quickies charging in
From half way to the screen and more
Expending energy galore.
It makes us off-break bowlers smile.
It's easier to bowl with guile.

How often has it proved the case
That batsmen who give stick to pace
Are next to hopeless with a spinner,
Scratching round like a beginner.
"Ten overs; six for twenty four-
He should have brought me on before!".

When batters take a leg-side guard
To smack you through the off side, hard,
The one that "goes on with arm"
Bowled with dexterity and charm
Can, on it's day, be worth a million,
Spreading gloom in the pavilion.

A useful one to have in store
Starts the seam at "ten to four".
It drifts away, then, like a dream,
Sometimes nips back off the seam
In ratio of one in three.
If you can't read it, how can he?

Turn one sharply and you'll find
Doubt sown in the batsman's mind;
So pitch 'em up, no matter which.
Don't let him watch you off the pitch.
Strike before he can embark
On striking you all round the park.

Left-handers find the going tough
When offies bowl it in the rough.
They play for spin, but if they knew,
It's pitched up arm balls that get through.
We get 'em with a double whammy.
Serves 'em right for being scrammy.

When batsmen swing us round to leg
An "arm ball" bowled at middle peg,
Well pitched up and pushed through quick,
Should beat the bat and do the trick.
If it doesn't bowl him out,
L.B.W's worth a shout.

It's not as easy as it sounds,
Especially on well kept grounds
Where bumps are flattened with a roller
To offer nothing to the bowler.
Footmarks are your last resource
So make a few - unseen of course!

When I keep them on the sticks
Batsmen pick me up for six,
Straight, or over deep mid-wicket.
It all produces brighter cricket.
But if I try to bowl my "flipper,"
"Thank you Arty," says the skipper.

Our feel-good factors are enamoured
Of watching Swanny getting hammered.
It resurrects our sad demeanours
When he gets taken to the cleaners.
If he gets stick with all his stealth
I can't be quite so bad myself!

Over

It's not all idle fancy - it's the truth;
Cricket can be played beyond our youth.
Not as long as we would like perhaps
But long enough to satisfy most chaps.
Even if we're plump and over fifty
Not so muscular and not so nifty
Well past our sell-by-date, it's all the same,
It's usually not hard to get a game.

Despite our satisfaction with our play
There comes to every cricketer a day
When struggling with the physical requirement,
Reluctantly, he contemplates retirement.
It's not that we can't bat with grace and style
Or bowl off-spin with elegance and guile
Longevity at length must sadly yield
To failure to perform when in the field.

I lumber round the field with leaden shoes
Turning two's to three's and one's to two's.
There's nowhere where the skipper hasn't tried me:
He's running out of places he can hide me
Anywhere in close you'll likely find me
As long as there's another chap behind me!
I try to see myself as I'm perceived
But find the truth too cruel to be believed.

Gone are the days when one could go to sleep
While nonchalantly fielding in the deep
Letting the ball come to you while you charm it,
Then slowly bend and gently over-arm it.
"Attack the ball!" they cry, and "Get it in!"
Demented by their pressing need to win;
And then you suffer ultimate disgrace -
The skipper puts a youngster in your place!

Or if the ball's well struck to left or right
You stick your boot out, stretch with all your might,
But no one reckons you have really tried
Unless you launch yourself into "the slide",
Risking life and limb, and maybe more,
Chucking yourself around to save a four,
Putting your ageing body through the mill
And plastering your togs with chlorophyll.

We'd like, when we retire, to choose the day
But, in the end, selectors have their say.
We sense that we're superfluous and licked
When, week on week, we simply don't get picked.
We pack our kit and keep the match days free
But gradually it dawns on you and me
The local pub, TocH, and all the rest
Don't even want to use us as a guest.

The modem game has finally denied me
And fancy fielding utterly defied me.
I know I've got the expertise a-plonty
Apart from fielding a-la Twenty 20.
I've not done bad, I'm 70 goodness knows;
We have to bring the youngsters in I s'pose.
What's that? My phone- "Yes, Arthur is my name."
(Thinks!) Perhaps it's TocH offering me a game!

Pavilion in Winter

While soccer has its day and cricket sleeps,
The old pavilion its vigil keeps.
Made fast from wind and rain it is at best
A place for dogs to sniff and birds to rest.
An incidental thing, but to a few,
Surety in kind for better things to do.
Come: mend your path across this frosty field
And see what things of interest lie concealed.

"Unknown yet well known"; none yet all the same.
Cloned into likeness by a common game.
The changing rooms where lesser mortals might
Transform themselves to demi-gods in white.
Bench seats that lift to secretly provide
Compartments where a cricketer can hide
Metal scoreboard numbers, boundary flags,
Nets and stumps and heavy canvas bags.

And opposite, across the stud-plucked floor,
Beyond the glazed half-open kitchen door,
An ancient water heater, plug pulled out,
A folded dish cloth flung across its spout.
A brown enamel teapot, cups and spoons,
Exclusively for match day afternoons;
The helpers, with the players, snatched away
Like swallows with the ever shortening day.

Cold and silent, sunk within its walls
The echoes of a thousand summer calls.
Shouted batting orders, discontent,
Muffled curses, loud encouragement;
The heavy sound of boots on hollow boards,
And mock abuse that comradeship affords;
And in the nadir of these winter suns
The ghosts of cricket's long forgotten ones.

Should passers by imagine they have found
A park or council recreation ground
And wrongly think it offers, if you please,
A place for strawberry fairs or jamborees,
The wooden sentinel secures its peace
'Til cricket takes again its summer lease
And strangely driven folk, as strangely clad,
Resume their rituals with bat and pad.

Prep School Cricket

From the corner of my Pre-Prep room I could see the wicket
And watch the big boys from the Prep School playing proper cricket.
They bowled so fast, they threw so far, they all knew what to do.
I dreamed of playing cricket like them in a year or two.
The thought of wearing pads for batting filled me with delight
And, most of all, I'd look just like them kitted out in white.

I'd practiced with my brother drawing wickets on the wall.
Our bat was made of plastic and we used a tennis ball.
"What would you like for Christmas?" "A cricket ball," I said.
I took it everywhere I went and slept with it in bed.
I thought it was so beautiful I didn't want to use it.
I was afraid to play with it just in case I'd lose it.

Another birthday came and went; how slowly time went by.
I couldn't wait to get to Prep School – no need to ask me why.
My classroom changed, to my dismay I couldn't see the wicket.
At least I wouldn't get in trouble trying to watch the cricket.
Sometimes, in the afternoons, I'd watch it from a distance;
Then Father Time, the schoolboy's friend, came to my assistance.

I needed lots of things for Prep School, things to wear and use.
Some my parents bought without me, some they let me choose.
Cricket bats weren't on the list but I thought I'd try it,
Told my Dad I needed one and asked him if he'd buy it.
To my surprise he bought me one; you can never tell.
I should have told him that I needed pads and gloves as well!

The scene was set for work and play and as the years went by
Prep School cricket helped produce no happier boy than I.
The things I'd dreamed of long ago have gradually come true;
I've learned to bat, I've learned to bowl, I know just what to do.
I look the part, I pull my weight, I never ever shirk.
Is that a pre-prep watching me instead of doing his work?

Prodigy

For the Christening of a cricketer's son.

A special child, a special day
To launch him on his pilgrim way
Through toil and laughter, joy and sorrow.
We wish for him a bright tomorrow.

Little fingers, little toes.
Shall he play cricket? No-one knows.
So tiny now; what will he be?
Bradman once was small as he.

Time works miracles we know.
Great oaks from little acorns grow.
Those hands so tender and so small
May one day spin a cricket ball.

Lots to learn and to survive
Before his parents can contrive
To teach him how to throw and catch
And watch him in a cricket match.

So much of life is sorely spent
And his will be no different,
But cricket's fascinating powers
Shall sanctify his leisure hours.

May he be blessed with diligence
In his pursuit of excellence
And reap the cream of life's rewards
By leading England out at Lords.

Reflections

I bowl to my reflection in the outside kitchen door;
Then, switching to a batsman's role, I face myself once more.
Was ever bowler quite so subtle with his sleight of hand?
Or ever batter quite so quick to read & understand?
Such wealth of cricket expertise by subterfuge concealed
Deserts me from the moment that I step onto the field!

Revisited

How frequently while travelling 'round
We drive through places where
In days gone by we could be found
At the local cricket ground.
We check the time, our pulses bound;
We'll see if it's still there.

It was all so long ago
We wonder if we'll find it.
Instinct leads and off we go,
Left or right, we hardly know,
But there it is, we told you so,
The little church behind it.

We lean upon the low brick wall,
A lingering moment spare
To hear the sounds of bat on ball,
The loud appeals, the batsman's call,
No one hears the whisper fall;
"I used to play on there."

It warms the heart, it lightens care,
It does an old man good.
It's something cricketers can share
Revisiting the places where
A man can say "I played on there"
And fancy he still could!

Sackcloth and Ashes

English cricket buffs are cock-a-hoop.
Australians are crying in their soup.
Twenty-four years on we shall return
Proud custodians of that little urn.
Much to our surprise and their dismay
Australian cricket is in disarray;
Choppng, changing, fiddling with the team,
Their "Last Night of the Poms" was just a dream.

Australians play the "grade" but couldn't make it.
They've dished it out, let's see if they can take it.
"Well done Pommies" sticks in Aussie gizzards.
In cricket circles Oz has lost its wizards.
Recall Shane Warne? Perhaps he's lost his thunder.
Have they got no rising stars down under?
No-one with a "doosrah" or a"flipper";
No obvious replacement for the skipper?

Their native confidence has turned to doubt;
Our stars kept twinkling while their lights went out.
The rancour and the flak will soon begin.
Their press, as well as ours, will rub it in.
The Ashes lost at home! How can it be?
The land of hope and Crocodile Dundee
Has seen the trophy nicked by Bob the Builder
And let Britannia waltz off with Matilda!

But genuine cricket lovers nationwide
Should not rejoice to see an Aussie side
Reduced to optimistic impotence
With records tumbling down at their expense.
An Ashes series fires imaginations
And Aussie pride enhances confrontations.
For all the banter, cricketers respect them
And wait in hope for fate to resurrect them.

Scorebook

Time marches on, the years fly by, the seasons come and go;
The cricketer grows wistful, he's comforted to know
That should his memory grow dim as one day may his sight
One vital aspect of his life is down in black and white.
And while life's small achievements have seldom been rewarded
At least his exploits on the field are faithfully recorded.
Moments of exuberance, skill and graft and pain
By looking through the scorebook can be lived and lived again.

It has its limitations, its formulation such
That while it seems to tell you all it doesn't tell you much.
The scorers are anonymous, there is of course no mention
If he, whoever he might be, was paying ,much attention.
It tells us what we settled for and gives us little signs
So those who played, on looking back, can read between the lines.
Take all the 'RUN OUTS' it records, you almost can depend
On 'Inzamum ul Eddie' being down the other end.

Simply writing 'CAUGHT' won't help the reader to be knowing
How low, how high, how much it spun, how fast the ball was going.
'Caught Cowell' for instance can't convey the tension and the doubt,
The circling round beneath the ball, the scurrying in and out.
'Caught Garner' hides a sleight of hand no other catch surpasses,
Swooping low at short square leg, left-handed, without glasses.
'Caught Bradbury' sounds quite ordinary, rather sportsmanlike;
No mention of the jerking thumb and cries of "on yer bike!"

Batsmen like to see their scores but most of us it's true
Have had some luck on level pitches; made a run or two.
Good knocks here from Sykes and Waldorf, Keppler and Magoo
Every dog has had his day – even me and you.
So let the book fall open; see which page is thumbed
And guess which batsmen secretly to ego have succumbed.
Barry's ton and Lambo's fifty, Grumpy's ninety nine –
That's the grubbiest page of all, the fingerprints aren't mine.

Big scores down the batting order always rouse suspicion,
Like bowlers coming back to polish off the opposition,
Average boosters fancying an easy bowl or bat.
Thank goodness Captain Grumpy never does a thing like that!
He works hard for his averages like every skipper should;
The game is more important, that's why they're not so good.
The scorebook tells the story, protest with all your might,
It's no good arguing the toss, it's there in black and white.

"Bowled Salway's" rather meaningless, it can't begin to say
If it 'went on with the arm' or 'went the other way'.
If it beat him 'in the flight' or ' with a change of pace,
Or hit a bump which, truth to tell, it usually the case.
"Bowled Rayer" used to be confusing failing to discern
If he was bowling medium pace or trying to get some turn.
Here's an over, 'Single, Single, dot, dot, dot and then
Whoops – a six, that's when he tried his Chinaman again.

Those little Gallic chevrons look innocent enough
But batsmen often feel hard done by, getting out is tough.
Good decision? Up in front? Got a snick or hasn't he?
The scorebook won't explain the umpire's name was Macatasney.
Despite perceived injustice Mel or Barry do not linger
Or mutter rude obscenities when Trigger lifts the finger.
Our batsmen are exemplary; they don't wax loud or shameless
Or vandalise the changing room like one who shall be nameless.

While you are grinding the gerund or suffering as a Tutor
Cowlly's in a little corner with his new computer.
The scorebook's open on his desk, he knows what he's about;
In go runs and wickets and our averages come out.
Perhaps some players haven't done as well as you might think;
They're glad it's cricket that we play and not 'The Weakest Link'.
Then – Crisis time – our scorebook, Cowlly's data base for ages,
Had itself been judged 'RUN OUT', we'd used up all the pages.

Trigger's brand new scorebook was greeted with euphoria
Despite the fact it's dated for the reign of Queen Victoria.
It's all a bit confusing but the payers at least will know
They weren't around to play the game a hundred years ago.
As Trigger's book is slowly filled some players who never knew him
A debt of gratitude will owe anonymously to him;
And though the dates are slightly wrong a scorebook's never boring
And a hundred out is not a lot when Trigger does the scoring.

Side-on

Like ladies in long skirts with horses to ride on
Cricket's a game that is best addressed side-on.
As shelves in a library, trains in a station,
Scope is enhanced by a side elevation.

That first big step forward is managed with ease,
Your back foot still safely ensconced in the crease;
And ducking the bouncers if that is your mission,
If simply performed if you stick to tradition

Some batsmen don't stand as they taught us at school
But they are exceptions for proving the rule.
Good bowlers can read your best shots in your stance
So face up side-on and don't give them the chance.

A side-on approach is considered the norm
When completing a risk assessment form.
It shields vital organs, the heart and the belly,
And cossets the parts they don't show on the telly.

Bad habits creep in as a player grows older,
So, always remember, look over your shoulder.
Batting or bowling the mantra's the same;
"Front shoulder round" is the name of the game.

You might not be Bradman, Tendulkar, or May,
But if you face up in a similar way
If everything fails that your image relied on
At least, for a while, you looked the part side-on!

Straight Blade

Style and natural talent play their part
But batting's not a science, it's an art.
Each innings is intrinsically unique,
A blend of innovation and technique,
Attention paid to one thing in particular;
The blade should be presented perpendicular.

Swing and spin we do our best to guess
But bounce, an honest batsman must confess,
Is quite beyond his power to predict.
This simple fact persuades us to be strict
And cover any lack of elevation
By ruling out all trace of inclination.

Our families present their maker's name
And at the crease our bats should do the same.
In cricket as in life, as well we might,
Strive to get the fundamentals right.
The mantra is, good batsmen always knew it;
"It's not just what you do, it's how you do it."

While others seem to prosper there's no doubt
When good balls come a straight bat keeps them out.
So keep your elbow up, your shoulder round
And , like as not, as many players have found,
As sloggers shoulder arms and leave the square
The man who plays it straight will still be there.

Team Kit Bag

A cricket bag's a splendid thing for any team to own,
Exuding possibilities and pure testosterone.
Famous victories, golden moments, feats with bat & ball,
Humiliation, ecstasy, the bag has shared them all.
We never even loiter when the skipper wants to lift it;
It takes a pair of supermen to pick it up & shift it.
It's not that we're unhelpful, selfish or chicken hearted;
We just don't want to bust a gut before the match has started.

Our bag is green & made of canvas, strong and leather bound,
Overfilled with kit we've purchased, borrowed, begged or found;
Emptied out on summer evenings when it doesn't rain,
But frankly half the stuff it holds we'll never use again-
Worn out gloves with pimply rubber stitched up to the knuckles,
Floppy pads with leather straps & little jingly buckles,
All marked 'Brookfield School' in pen in prominent positions,
And some with names of other clubs, nicked from the opposition.

A small pink box comes popping out as if as much to say,
'Which one of you will take a chance & put me on today?'
You may have seen (of course you have – I'm surely not alone)
That all the serious cricketers have boxes of their own,
What do they know that we don't? Perhaps we should take steps
To get the things inspected by the Health & Safety reps.
One ponders possibilities too gross to contemplate;
Have they been washed since they were bought in 1988?

Old cricket balls are everywhere without a hint of gloss
And shiny new ones, tissue wrapped, in case we win the toss.
But what's this ghastly yellow thing? It's really quite beyond us.
If it is a cricket ball has it got yellow jaundice?
The skipper got it on the net with matching mobile phone;
It's quite bizarre, he's gone too far – I'm leaving it alone.
I bet it came from Vegas or even the Bahamas;
If the skipper had his way we'd all play in pyjamas!

Here's a funny squidgy thing; goodness knows what this is.
Judging by the feel of it it's something for the cissies.
Chaps who get the collywobbles facing up to bumpers,
Stuff 'em down their trouser legs or shove 'em up their jumpers.
With some of these about their persons chaps aren't what they seem
And finish up resembling a Yankee football team.
If ever Brian Close felt need to cosset life and limb,
A copy of the 'Yorkshire Post' was good enough for him.

Certain items in the bag are prized above the rest
And 'jack-men' rush to grab them first & guarantee the best;
The pukkha gloves, the newest pads, the V200 bat.
Only 'wickies' get their own but no one fancies that.
We're getting near the bottom now, the canvas sides that bulged
Lie flat like a deflated balloon, their secrets all divulged -
Stumps & scorebooks, bails and boxes, various utensils,
Stones for umpires, blades of grass, and broken scorer's pencils.

But search among the contents & I doubt you will discover
A little book with 'Laws of Cricket' written on the cover,
For guidance of the wise & the obedience of fools
Surely, perforce, we need recourse to such a book of rules.
But no-one could ever, however clever, begin to anticipate
The comedy of errors we consistently create.
We don't play cricket by the book, the situation's this -
When all is done, we play for fun, & ignorance is bliss.

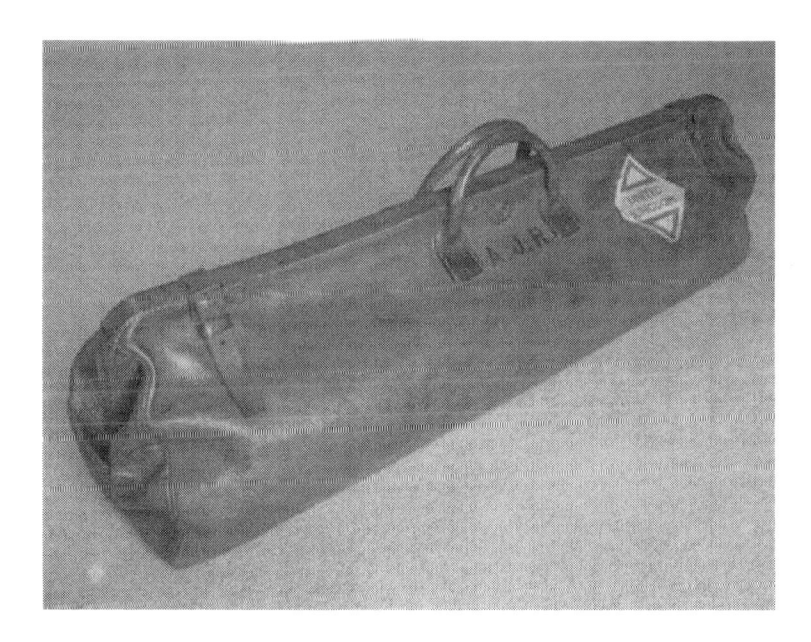

The Amateurs

Gone are the days when men of means & measure
Bestrode county cricket grounds for pleasure,
Their talents sought unpurchased it would seem,
Their skill uncoached, their status their regime.
Some, by their naked flair, had earned their station
Apart from influence and obligation;
While others in those early days of paucity,
Ensured selection by their generosity.

Every county fielded one or two
And no-one dared to tell them what to do.
"Can't make the nets this week old chap – I'm sorry".
"That's quite alright Sir; thank you. Please don't worry."
One wonders how an Amateur would greet
A call for him to get up on his feet
And march into the middle with the drinks:
Hardly a "bonding exercise" methinks!

In fact, in pre-war English county cricket
A "pro" as skipper wasn't quite the ticket.
The Amateurs were captains, by adoption,
And serving drinks, for them, was not an option.
They were, of course, quite wealthy as a rule
But some were teachers 'down' from Public School
And likely, if they didn't get their bat in,
To tell the umpire off in Greek or Latin.

Some stayed aloof, but there were surely those
Who minimised the protocol and chose
Through laughter and encouragement on the field
To push those barriers which, in time, would yield;
Barriers that were slowly disappearing
Aided by cricket's social engineering.
And while it always mattered that they won,
The "pros" earned money while the Amateurs had fun.

Long gone those cavalier aristocrats;
Their gaudy blazers, caps, and flashing bats.
They brought a whiff of license to the crease
That payment or reward cannot release.
Perhaps the English county scene has lost
Much more than their benevolence has cost.
"Good riddance", say those folk who never knew them;
And painful were the throes that overthrew them.

They're still around, of course, on some committee;
But never at the wicket – what a pity!

The Cameo

The batsman shrugs and leaves the crease
Reluctantly, and ill at ease.
The scorer turns; is heard to say,
"Old Mel was looking good today".
The chevrons go against his name;
No comfort that it's just a game
The long walk back with shoulders bent
Desiring no acknowledgement.
No ripple please, no "Bad luck" call;
Faint praise is worse than none at all.
The bowlers' heads were down & shaking,
The runs were surely there for the taking.
A three, a four, and then another;
A well judged two to extra cover
Then- caught & bowled; it must be said
It should have gone above his head.

Batsman; ignore the faint applause.
Remember this to help your cause;
Some men too old to play at all
And boys who will but are too small
Enjoyed those runs for their true worth;
A part of English summers' mirth.

The Commentators

Before the advent of T.V.
Brought images that we could see
We were virtual spectators
Courtesy of commentators.
They were our eyes who witnessed all
And what they said was what we saw.

No levity, no friendly jibe;
Their brief was simply to describe.
Arlott, Alston, Peter West,
Raymond Baxter and the rest
Described each stroke (it could be boring)
While Roy Webber did the scoring.

E.W. Swanton, alias "Jim";
How many can remember him?
"It's catch and bowled" was what he thought,
His syntax good but rather fraught.
Never a man to raise a laugh,
"Jim"Swanton of the Telegraph

John Arlott was a different fellow,
His voice bucolic, warm and mellow.
He'd charm his listeners for hours
With his quaint descriptive powers.
Old words seemed like new to us –
"That cut was almost posthumous!"

If scenarios made you happy
Henry Blofeld was your chappie,
Cricket's Prince of rabble rousers;
Kitsch bow-tie and scarlet trousers.
"There goes a bus on the Radcliffe Road.
Woops! My toddy's overflowed."

When T.V. came upon the scene
(or p'raps vice versa's what I mean)
No longer was the commentator
Our vicarious spectator.
Descriptions were superfluous.
What could the fellows say to us?

Their role must change, and in the main,
The brief was now to entertain.
Exit Messers West and Swanton;
Enter Mr. Brian Johnston;
Bonhomie and lovely grub,
President of the Riff-raff Club.

Nicknames followed lightening toil;
"Blowers," "Aggers," "Bothers," "Boil."
The studio was, as a rule,
Like break-time at a Public School.
Innuendo, puerile pleasure
And chocolate sponge cake for good measure.

All of which is fine you see
If you are watching on T.V;
But some who listen to the cricket
Think it isn't quite the ticket
Cracking jokes and remonstrating
When they should be commentating.

But if we're honest, most I guess
Are avid fans of T.M.S.
We love the stats, the banter too;
Even Yorkshire's "You-know-who."
And if we want the state of play
We can rely on C.M.J.

So thank you gents for all your words
From Trent Bridge, Headingly and Lord's,
In company or all alone
With your little microphone
Swatting wasps and sweating streams
To help us visualise our dreams.

The Cricket Field

Fortunate indeed this field;
It's destiny is not to yield
A harvest made with wheat and corn
From rutting plough or harrow born,
But cleared of lump & stump & thicket
Is set aside for playing cricket.

In winter gentle sheep may graze
Preserving turf for summer days,
A picket fence thrown round the square
Should hoof or human trespass there.
Some say we should share – use the land-
Clearly, they don't understand.

This field shall always take its name
Only from England's noblest game.
Despite its level disposition
And most favourable condition
Hockey posts shall not be found,
This is no recreation ground.

Four generations, maybe more,
Since long before the first World War,
Cricketers long gone, & some
Who play today, & those to come,
All sow unmixed the seeds of cricket
And harvest only run & wicket.

The Cricket Widow

The scene is set. Let joy be unconfined
And let us celebrate with heart and mind
This day that brings horizons bright and new;
The day that sees her childhood dreams come true.
No time for gloom, you say, no place for tears,
And yet the blushing bride has inward fears
And ponders amid all that's bright and good
The prospect of impending widowhood.

"Widowhood?" you cry, "What are you saying?
What deadly game of bluff is this girl playing?
Does she have plans to do her husband in
 Before he even gets a chance to sin?"
She must be raving bonkers or delirious.
As McEnroe would say, "You can't be serious!"
But then, as many fellas have been warned,
"Hell hath no fury like a woman scorned."

If there's another passion in his life
What future is there for his suffering wife?
What kind of girl could gladly tie the knot
Aware of competition that she's got;
Another love, a rival for his heart
To keep him from her, claim a major part
In all he plans to do, now and for ever.
Is such a marriage really very clever?

Relax dear friends. There's no cause for concern.
No doubt you'll all be gratified to learn
The competition comes not from a dame
But from our most seductive English game.
It's not that hubby won't be quite the ticket.
It's just that he's addicted to his cricket,
And if his life pursues its current trends
She'll only be a widow at week-ends.

When the time had come to name the day
Prospective husband phoned the Skip to say
He'd be otherwise engaged and couldn't make it
And wondered how on earth the chap would take it.
"O.K. old man", he said, "we'll overlook it.
Thanks for ringing up before you book it.
We'll let you off to have your little fun day.
I'll text you if we're desperate on the Sunday!"

Next day the Skipper rang him back to ask
If he could help to simplify the task.
Was there, he wondered, really any reason
Why they couldn't marry out of season.
"Put it off a month or two," he said,
"December is a cosy time to wed.
Besides, the team could all be in your pictures
Without the need to cancel any fixtures."

She knows she'll be expected , if you please,
To keep the score or help out with the teas,
And when the cricket matches are "away"
He'll want to "socialise," or so he'll say.
That means to drink his socks off at the bar
While she drinks Cokes so she can drive the car.
No way Jose! He's better on his jack;
And she'll be fast asleep when he gets back!

She's doomed to spend her Saturdays alone;
Watching telly, chatting on the phone,
Deprived of all those things a wife enjoys
While he's off chasing leather with the boys.
Not many newly-weds can claim that they
Became a widow on their wedding day.
But that's the score. I reckon she can stick it,
As long as he is only playing cricket!

The English Game

Close your eyes – picture the scene
The pub, the church, the village green,
Flannelled figures round the wicket,
This is England, this is cricket.
Even non – cricketers confess
Its quintessential Englishness.
It is, for those in any doubt,
What two world wars were all about;
Peace on earth and God in Heaven-
Tea time, 156 for 7

In days of Empire, days of yore,
In Timbuktu and Bangalore
We taught the natives how to play it
And now; I hesitate to say it,
Home or away, no matter where
They stuff us with a day to spare.
Administrators swallow pride
And vie to get them in their side.
At county grounds whichever venue
Scorecards read more like a menu.

Take our current "England team"
Alas things are not what they seem.
You'd think from over 50 million
We could put in the pavilion
Eleven players, even ten,
Genuine true-born Englishmen.
What a cosmopolitan bunch;
You wonder what they have for lunch!
The only thing they have in common is
They learned their cricket in the colonies.

Gone the days, and what a shame,
When an England player had an English name
Like Larwood, Washbrook, Smith or Compton,
Born in Bradford, Bath or Brompton.
(Now he's born in Notty Ash, but his name is, Ramprakash.)
And Smithy wasn't English was he?
And even Craig White is an Aussie.
Hick waited years to qualify;
Now I expect he wonders why.

Many an English boy would dream
Of leading out the England team;
But recent history records
Foreigners in charge at Lords.
The choice of captain must be wise
Showing no racial compromise
But selectors should distinguish
Between who is and isn't English,
Keeping the noblest job in cricket
Away from those not quite the ticket.

But, on the contrary, what they do is
Give the job to Tony Lewis
Then in a show of rare largesse
Pass it on to Mike Denness;
One a Welshman, one a Scot.
Did we like if? Not a lot.
"British" isn't "English" really,
We were happiest with Brearley.
Then English cricket hit the dregs;
What captaincy was worse than Greig's?
Who, to make a crafty smacker,
Sold the team to Kerry Packer!

It's no good, getting sad and 'whingey',
We started it with Ranjit Sinji,
Glad to welcome and applaud
Talented ringers from abroad.
Purists may moan and curse about them,
We'd be even worse without them.
Perhaps selectors, if you please,
Should surf colonial family trees
And see if any likely lads
Were born to English mums or dads.

We don't need high-sounding orat'ry,
The future lies in the laborat'ry.
No excuses, no more moaning.
The M.C.C. must go for cloning.
Instead of making sheep or mutton
Clone a Compton or a Hutton,
Larwood, Botham, Maurice Tate,
Every English all-time great;
Challenge the Aussies and surprise'em
And hope they didn't recognise 'em.

Enough – the history book declares.
Our game's been good for world affairs.
Mandela owes, it would appear, a
Round of drinks to D'Olivera.
Lately there comes upon the scene
A chronicler named Benny Green
Whose book kicked up an awful stench
Suggesting that our game is French.
It's not. It's English, clear and plain;
Just like our Captain, Nasser Hussain!

The First Ball

The skipper allocates positions, trying hard to please;
Some for the athletic ones and some for refugees.
The bright new ball is tossed around and "kept up" to preserve it.
The fielders clap the batsmen in although they don't deserve it.
The wicket keeper bends his knees, the umpires take their station;
The scene is set, the cricket match awaits initiation.
The scorer's watching , pencil poised, the bowler's standing tall;
The waiting's over, "Game on chaps", it's time for the first ball.

It's like the launching of a ship, the opening of a fete,
And when it's done euphoria begins to dissipate.
The "loosener" is supposed to get the bowler in his stride
And batsmen look to watch it through if it's a trifle wide,
But then-on things are different, although you're having fun,
The next ball is more serious – the contest has begun.
It's time to get up on your toes and do what you are told.
What's different then? The difference is the 'first ball' has been bowled.

The bowler doesn't think it's 'just a loosener' at all;
So much depends on how it feels when bowling that first ball.
Have you marked your run up right? Are your boots OK?
Is it going to swing and is your radar right today?
And if you are the batsman you're wondering if he's fast,
And hoping that the first ball bowled won't also be your last.
You check your box, you check the field to see where you can knock it
But truth to tell, for starters, you'll be happy just to block it.

As time and overs trundle by and opening batsmen fall,
Each player coming in to bat must face his own 'first ball'.
He'll name his guard, he'll tap the crease, his life will flash before him:
He'll pray the 'Spirit of the Don' will suddenly come o'er him.
He might survive and then contrive to rattle up a ton,
But batsmen know, that fast or slow, you miss it – you get none.
And if the first ball gets you, on payment of a sub,
You qualify to go on-line and join the Primary Club.

Rational folk won't understand just how the 'first ball' is
An unassuming watershed between realities.
Work and worry, life and loves are temporarily suspended
To stay 'on hold' until the game reluctantly is ended.
The pitch is booked, the players summoned, many a phone call made,
Kit transported, weather fair, the match can now be played:
But the 'first ball' is the gambit that bids the best man win,
And states in shining leather – let the fantasy begin.

The Nightwatchman

For week-end cricketers like me and you
It's not a thing we're called upon to do.
Our games are done and dusted on the day;
If you ask me by far the better way
To bring a cricket match to its conclusion
Without the need for overnight confusion.
Being the "Night Watchman" is no joke
And not a fate I'd wish on any bloke.

It's not what bowlers have in mind at all.
You live in hope you'll never get the call.
Batting isn't really your concern;
You do your best, you have to take your turn.
Then, suddenly, you're asked to be tenacious,
Rather like a cricketing Horatius.
Only an Ancient Roman or a Scotsman
Would back himself at being the "Night Watchman."

The perils are concealed; it is a trap
That can ensnare an unsuspecting chap.
The light is awful but you can't refuse.
You just can't win; you're guaranteed to lose.
Do it badly and you get the blame
For setting them on course to lose the game.
Do it well you get applause, but then
You'll find yourself the "Night Watchman" again

Two batsmen at the crease, but of the two
If anyone gets out it must be you.
Runs don't matter but who cares, by heck,
With half their fielders breathing down your neck.
They're calling up their Asian mystery spinner.
He'll have you scratching round like a beginner.
Your sole objective is to soak up sorrow
So Smartypants is there to bat tommorrow.

And if you do your stuff and see out time
When morning comes they'll see it as a crime
If you don't slog and sacrifice your wicket.
It isn't fair; it simply isn't cricket.
No self respecting chap should be put through it.
At least the pros are getting paid to do it.
Being a "Night Watchman's" not my scene;
I'll stick to cricket on the village green!

The Old Ball

If you should go to my bureau your eye would surely fall
Upon an unexpected thing; a worn out cricket ball.
It's charms are wasted on my wife, she'll never understand
Why I should keep the useless thing and take it in my hand
My first and second fingers placed, as far as I can see,
As demonstrated by the late Jim Laker on T.V.
In my mind I see it flighted, flutt'ring in the breeze,
Pitching fair and turning square across the batsman's knees.

It's newness thrilled the opening bowlers; tantalised the spinners;
A thing of joy for man and boy, for experts or beginners,
Hard and shiny, gold-embossed on deep luxurious red
Nestling like a ruby in its tissue paper bed,
Carrying our hopes and fears for vict'ry or for loss
Hidden in the skipper's bag in case he wins the toss.
It's pristine beauty faded fast with every run they scored,
Its shape knocked out by many a clout from bat and boundary board.

It suffered for or pleasure and bears the scars of glory.
The scorebook gives statistics but the old ball tells the story.
Is this the ball that Lambo smote, that Waldorf saved the side with?
That Eddie stopped and Cowlly dropped and Grumpy bowled a wide with?
That Barry lofted hard and high for a majestic six
And Westell split his pants to reach swooping behind the sticks.
Each stroke has left its imprint, each flaw a man betraying.
Judging from the well picked seam, "You-know-who" was playing!

Old cricketers get worn out too, just like my cricket ball.
The day will come when we're replaced and never used at all.
We gradually deteriorate, our speed and skills decline.
I'm conscious of your waning form, you're more aware of mine.
The game is over when we bowl, as batsmen we're neglected.
The skipper hides us in the field – that's if we get selected!
"Only fit for practice" is the message in the ball
So if you're forty-five or more, the writing's on the wall

We salute you worn-out ball. As anyone can see
You've years of cricket left in you as, obviously, have we!

The Pavilion End

The sightscreen slightly to his right
Old Tom enjoys a perfect sight
Of swing and bounce and turn and flight
At the pavilion end

He never sits beneath the tree:
True cricketers should always be
Behind the 'arm where they can see
At the pavilion end

The bowling might as well be wide
To those who watch it from the side
Thank goodness they have never tried
At the pavilion end

Next-in batsmen come to say
"What's the bowling like today?"
The teapot's never far away
At the pavilion end

Time was when he would turn his arm
With guile, variety and charm
But now he sits beyond all harm
At the pavilion end

Some day when things are not the same
A wooden bench shall bear his name –
"Tom Brown, who always watched the game
At the pavilion end".

Picture the scene -

A small country cricket ground "somewhere in England". As the church clock strikes "two", cars begin to arrive & the drivers, some already in whites, greet each other noisily. Doors slam, boots open to disgorge chairs & cricket bags; ladies carry tins, jugs and cloth covered trays into the small wooden pavilion.

A mobile phone rings and the resulting conversation causes alarm. Cars arrive regularly now and a tall fit-looking stranger approaches the man with the phone. It is a moment pregnant with possibility-

he is:-

The Ringer

A sunny day in August, just the kind of day you'd choose
To play the match between St. Pauls & St. Bartholemews;
And one of those coincidences not unknown in sport
Produced a "ringer" with his kit the day we were one short.
Someone asked him what he did, "All rounder" he replied.
"Just the job" the skipper chuckled, "Welcome to the side.
We like to win but basically it's all a bit of fun;
I've won the toss so pad up quick & go in number one".

Our bells have long been silent so strange as it may seem
The only ringer at St. Bart's was in the cricket team.
He'd played in Minor Counties, for Cowfordshire no less,
Be sure that we, as well as he, were anxious to impress,
To kid him on we knew our stuff, to try to look the part,
But truth to tell we'd blown our cover long before the start;
We'd brought our little canvas bags to shove our bits of kit in,
But Ringer's massive fibre box was big enough to sit in.

He'd pads & gloves & chest protectors, bats from which to choose,
Helmets, caps & velcro straps like real professionals use.
The opposition trotted out anticipating play
Innocently throwing catches unaware that they
Would soon be suffering in the sun, their hopes of victory dashed;
The Ringer would ensure that they were well & truly thrashed.
We all feel rather guilty, it didn't seem quite fair,
But they had stuffed us last time round & now we'd all be square.

He watched a couple, blocked a couple, pushed one through the off,
Then smashed a soaring six, like Ballesteros playing golf.
They took an age to find it, bottoms up amid the clover,
While a startled looking umpire, left the field to move his Rover.
Their captain changed his field around, all credit to the chap,
But where the fielder used to be, the Ringer found the gap.
It seems hilarious at the time, but how were we to know
How we would be embarrassed, by the way events would go.

The opening bowler'd had enough and took his massive bulk
To deep - mid - backward - nowhere to lick his wounds & sulk,
The Vicar, summoned with a wave, came in from short fine leg
To bowl his loopy dolly mixtures aimed at middle peg.
Ringer showed him scant respect & slammed him hard & high -
"There's one for the missionaries", we clearly heard him cry;
And then for 62 for nought, attempting one six more,
Was given L.B.W. – stood his ground and swore.

"Well played", called the skipper in an effort to diffuse
The tension building on the square; it was a timely ruse.
We clapped & cheered until the Ringer left the crease at last
Saying something nasty to the umpire as he passed.
He stumped into the changing room & slammed the door behind him.
"A guest", the skipper shouted out, "you really mustn't mind him".
First wicket down was just preparing to address the ball
When Ringer threw his Duncan Fearnley through the toilet wall.

"Good grief," the skipper mumbled, "I think I'd better start
To try and calm him down before he takes the place apart."
At tea we mingled well enough, apologies were made;
The bad taste ling'ring in our mouths was not the lemonade.
The Ringer laughed and joked with us & with the opposition;
He seemed a friendly sort of chap when not in competition.
I asked "Why can't he take it like a normal fellow would?"
The skipper said that if he did he wouldn't be so good.

Their innings started brightly, they were soon on course to get
The one-four-six to win that St. Bartholomew's had set.
Running like an antelope and throwing like a gun
The Ringer was at cover point & third man all in one.
The wickie couldn't cope with him & took some painful blows
While fielders chucked themselves around to stop the overthrows.
At 27 overs gone and 95 for 2
The skipper waved the Ringer up to show what he could do.

By now all thoughts of victory were tempered by our fears
That Ringer's contribution would make it end in tears
He placed his field decisively with ominous precision.
The skipper asked for back-stop but was greeted with derision.
We all stood rooted to the spot, half afraid to move
In case we wandered out of place and Ringer disapprove.
He'd put me by a fag-end in between two lumps of clover:
I prayed to God I'd find it at the end of the next over.

He'd said he was a spinner & he spun the ball t'was true,
But we were flabbergasted at the speed he pushed them through.
The wickie couldn't read him which to us was no surprise
But Ringer wasn't happy when so many went for byes.
Fine leg starting drifting round; it seemed the place to go,
But Ringer waved him back again with signs we didn't know.
The skipper chuntered in the slips, the wickie chuntered too.
The next one was the 'arm ball' & the wickie let it through.

Words were not required for the Ringer to convey
His message to the wickie on the standard of his play.
"Over", called the umpire & we all reflected that
Of all the seven runs it cost not one was off the bat.
The skip took wicket number three, a stumping if you please,
And to a ripple of applause the Vicar took the crease.
He'd played 'played a bit in India' we'd always understood
And though his limbs were knocking on his eye was pretty good.

He seemed to read the Ringer & with shots around the square
The green shoots of a cameo were definitely there.
An 'arm ball' found the outside edge & looped towards the slips
Where Chief Inspector Howard stood his hands upon his hips.
He dived, he groped, he lost his cap, he finished on the floor;
The ball he knew he should have caught went bobbling on for four.
At once this ageing pillar of the Dampfordshire Constabulary
Became the subject of the Ringer's colourful vocabulary.

"Easy" called the skipper quickly sensitive to shame.
"Yes", enjoined the Vicar, "just remember it's a game".
The Ringer mumbling as he turned, ran in towards the Vicar;
Some balls he'd bowled before were fast, but this was three times quicker.
It beat the back defensive stroke and violently connected
With part of the anatomy that should have been protected.
The Vicar, crouched for comfort, said, "I'm sorry, I can't help it"
Speaking with sincerity not managed from the pulpit.

The Vicar tried to carry on, In fact there was some doubt
If he was praying to stay in or praying to get out.
If it was the latter & he sought relief from care
The next ball from the Ringer brought the answer to his prayer.
He left to heartening applause but looking rather glum;
We hoped he didn't see the Ringer gesture with his thumb.
The next man wore trousers, not flannels like he should
And gullible as ever we assumed he was no good.

He soon suggested otherwise with boundaries off the skipper
And six into the graveyard when the doctor bowled his 'flipper'.
They only needed twenty now & didn't need to hurry
But with the Ringer bowling through we didn't need to worry.
Appealing like a banshee with the whole team round the bat
He stumped the last man backing up, we'd won and that was that.
We'd lost last year & hung around, they didn't do the same;
Even though we'd won the match we knew we'd lost the game.

You might suppose it boosts morale & celebrates our cause
To take sadistic pleasure from the way we stuffed St. Pauls,
In fact the opposite is true, the Ringer in his way
Had shown the cost of victory was more than we could pay.
We've lost the fixture sadly & there the matter rests;
Perhaps it's just as well in case they cram their team with guests.
But one thing's pretty certain, whatever else befalls,
We won't forget the Ringer, & neither will St. Pauls!

The Skipper

His the task of conjuring a side
From players often scattered far and wide.
The pitch, the ball, the carriage of the kit,
The teas, the transport; he arranges it.
In all he must succeed beyond all blame
And finally contrive to win the game

Take Saturday, we bowl them out by "three".
The skipper smiles, "Well played my lads," says he.
"Ninety six all out should see us right.
It's early drinks for everyone tonight."
Faced with a score that guarantees a win
He wisely hides his troubles with a grin.

A subtle frown disturbs his sun-kissed brow.
His problem is not if we win but how.
To win discreetly from a strong position
Without offending humble opposition;
To play to win but always to exalt
The game above its ultimate result.

He'd used effective bowlers much too soon.
How can he make it last the afternoon?
Promote tail-enders; let them go in first.
Push Arty up the order – he's the worst.
Eddie's bragging on about his hat-trick
So put him down and open up with Patrick.

And so unfolds the skipper's master plan.
Knowing the skills and foibles of each man
He chops and changes to achieve his aim,
To manufacture something from the game
One hard-learned lesson always uppermost
That none will praise him if the game is lost.

Sensing hopes and fears at every station
And using lesser players for compensation
The interval for tea is safely passed.
The skipper's coming to the crease at last
The game securely poised beyond all doubt
With Patrick stuck on seventeen not out.

A "two," a "one," a no-ball if you please
And Brookfield win without apparent ease.
The skipper's happy; only Eddie's vexed.
He's just got padded up to come in next.
Some might have thought we nearly didn't nick it.
That's how it's done. That's captaincy. That's cricket!

The Toss

It's quaint, and rather English too,
This thing that cricket captains do,
Chucking a coin up in the air
Assuming that the outcome's fair;
Committed to succeed or fail
By simply calling "head" or "tail".

On village greens, no worse for that,
The team a couple short will bat
So play can start without embarrassment,
No borrowed fielders, boys, or harassment.
The message is quite simple mate –
You want to chase? – Don't turn up late!

Serious captains one and all
Observe this honoured ritual,
Spinning a coin out in the middle
To see who's going to get first diddle;
And many a Tests' been won or lost
By the skippers call when the penny's tossed.

Bradman, Hammond, Mike Denness,
Benaud, Jardine and the rest,
All have stood and watched and waited
While that little coin gyrated,
Wishing that they somehow knew
What the blooming thing would do.

"What do they use?" we ask ourselves,
Special coins kept on the shelves
And dusted off as requires,
Duly presented to the umpires?
In fifty years what then? – who knows?
They'll flip a credit card I s'pose!

Although it isn't very clever
We can't help wondering if ever
England's heroes have resorted
To tossing coins when feeling thwarted.
Wellington at Waterloo
Probably tossed a crown or two.

And Nelson – should he go on deck
Or stay below and save his neck?
Up top his crew would cheer and salute him
But then some Frenchie might just shoot him.
Was a golden guinea tossed?
If so, I rather think he lost.

Those on the Parliamentary scene,
Even Her Majesty the Queen
Have they, when facing grave decisions,
Requiring statesmanship and vision
Risked our national well-being
And solved it quickly with a shilling?

We've won the toss! We'll have first crack
So put that brand new cherry back
And swap it for the old one meant
For use in such a rare event.
Never mind they're two men light –
Well done skip – you got it right!

The skipper breaks the news that you are No.11 with such comments as. "I have decided to hold you back" or "I want to strengthen the lower order"; both of which mean that in his opinion you, of all the players, are least likely to profit from time spent at the crease.

Your eventual arrival at the wicket is the signal for joke bowlers to be summoned from the deep wearing jeans, logo tee shirts, and if at all possible, Yogi Bear hats (reversed). They proceed to bowl unhittable deliveries which you humiliatingly try to reach.

Alternatively a demon bowler with overs left pounds in to enhance his averages. Your partner sees you as standing between him and glory and runs you ragged. However it is viewed it is a doubtful privilege to be:-

The Ultimate Batsman

As you watched the wickets fall
You saw the writing on the wall
Are you happy? Not at all
Last man.

The skip says, "Take it nice and steady",
He boosts your ego, unlike Eddie –
He's changed and in his car already
Last man.

Epitomising melancholy
You walk out feigning to be jolly.
Actually you feel a wally.
Last stand.

The ball is 30 overs old,
You've got to do as you are told,
Your gloves are warm and your box is cold,
Last chance

They're going to stuff us – what a shame.
Last week it was just the same.
You plan to play your natural game.
Last fling.

It's all the middle order's fault,
They should have batted as they ought,
But Mel was bowled and Bas was caught,
Last hope.

They come in close and clap you in
You stand between them and a win
The cabaret can now begin.
Last laugh.

All semblance of a match has gone,
They bring the cartoon bowlers on,
Sixty runs off twenty one.
Last wish.

He bowls a wide; can't even nick it,
Your partner's halfway down the wicket
Screaming "One" – this isn't cricket;
Last gasp.

Forty runs off thirteen balls,
Run like hell whoever calls,
Your average is in decimals.
Last over.

When he's on strike he wants a "two",
He's not a better bat than you,
But what can tail-end-Charlie do?
Last ball.

Your partner drives, you hear him curse;
Straight to cover – goodnight nurse.
You kept your end up; could be worse.
Last word.

You change alone and here's the rub,
By the time you reach the pub,
They've eaten nearly all the grub.
Last straw.

Tragedy at St. Helen's

It's best, perhaps, it's not for us to know
The time, the place, the manner we shall go.
We have no opportunity to choose
Nor ours an option that we may refuse.
But could we gentle Providence persuade
That darkest hours be somehow brighter made;
No fears, no pain, no suffering or remorse,
That life's last stumblings happen in the course
Of pleasant pathways walked with many a friend.
So may we come at last to journey's end.

And so it was. His umpire's task was done,
His eyes still shielded from the passing sun,
The counting stones divided in his hand.
We miss, we mourn, we try to understand.
We would not strive to keep what we must lose
Nor take from him what we ourselves would choose.
Now other men must do as once he would,
Standing white-coated where he lately stood;
And cricket, Alcwyn's lifelong, wise tutorial
Shall be, in its continuance, his memorial.

In July 2009, at St. Helen's, Swansea, umpire Alcwyn Jenkins was struck by a ball thrown in from the outfield and died at the scene. The South Wales Cricket Association requested a poem to be read at the funeral. It is included in this collection in his memory.

Umpiring

Some rather fancy umpiring; I can't see why they rate it.
Some even make their living at it. Personally I hate it.
Standing out there in the sun adjudicating bumpers,
Sweltering in a duvet of discarded woolly jumpers.
Applying laws and counting balls, and concentrating hard,
Signalling to the scorer chap and giving blokes their guard.

I think I know the signals. They should provide a giggle;
Especially my "four-scored" with its wiggle-wiggle-wiggle.
I live in hope that some poor dope, before I get much older
Will be a sport and run "one-short" so I can touch my shoulder.
And there's another signal that should cause a bit of fun;
I've got to hop around a bit when we reach one-one-one.

I've got my little bits of stone to register each ball.
I can count to six of course; I don't need them at all.
But umpires always use them, no matter where it is;
Watch T.V. and you will see old Dickie Bird with his.
"Over bowled!" The stones have gone. What's all the shouting for?
What do they mean, "- forgot the wide, we've got to have one more?"

Left-handers are a bloomin' pain it cannot be denied,
Making fielders chop and change and flit from side to side.
I don't see why I should comply; I see no logic in it.
We all know, that if I go, I'm back her in a minute.
I have one over-riding reason not to make the movement.
I'll see their ears and not their rears. A definite improvement!

L.B.W.'s difficult. There's always room for doubt;
And have you met the batsman who'll admit that he was out?
The better players are the worst. It wounds their sporting pride.
They shake their heads, they touch their bats, they point to either side.
They try to make you change your mind in any way they can,
Then -   what was that he said to me? The nasty little man!

"Caught-behind" is dodgy too. The ball goes whistling past.
A swish, a click, a diving catch. It's happening so fast.
Was it his bat, was it his pad, that made that snicking noise?
It's snap decisions, quickly made, that sort out men from boys.
I'll say "Not out!" There is some doubt. There always is when hooking.
It's worth a shout. He might be out. I'd know if I'd been looking

"Run-out" is a tricky one. The proper thing to do
Is move away so you can say you had a perfect view.
He hits to leg, you move to off – it's done with such precision;
The fruit of vast experience of many a tight decision.
Good grief! The skipper's cut it fine. "Ow 'zat?" the fielders shout.
"-Afraid I was unsighted chaps. I'll have to say `Not-out`".

Was he L.B.W.? Did it pitch outside?
Did the bowler overstep? Shall I call a wide?
Has the ball gone out of shape? Is that middle peg?
Have they got too many fielders round behind square leg?
We do our best. You blokes protest. You've every cause to doubt us.
We do our bit, you must admit. Where would you be without us?

What's in a Name

What's in a name? What difference can it make?
Who cares what something's called for goodness sake?
So why, when names are changed, are folk offended
And so much time and energy expended
In private fumings, angst, and protestation
And public demonstrations of frustration?

The emblem that for years our county side
Has taken to its heart and worn with pride
At Dean's Park, Portsmouth, even at May's Bounty,
Is spurned at the headquarters of the county.
In our darkest dreams who could suppose
That mammon should supplant the "Hampshire Rose"?

Of course we're pleased to see some funding banked
But sell the "Rose"? Is nothing sacrosanct?
A rose has charm and fragrance to intrigue us,
There's nothing beautiful about an Ageas..
"The Ageas Bowl," (we hate to seem ungrateful),
 Is still "The Rose Bowl" to the Hampshire faithful.

As part of a sponsorship deal the name of Hampshire's home ground was changed. It brought the "grumpy old men" out of the woodwork.

Why?

Why do boys love cricket? Why indeed.
It satisfies a youngsters growing need
For conquest, order, comradeship and skill
That other sports and pastimes can't fulfil.
So much to master, ponder, and admire
To which, in early years, they may aspire.
An adult world that beckons at its door
For those who can to share in its rapport
With pads, pavilions, googlies, and flight
And wear the uniform of gleaming white.

Why do men love cricket as they do?
They chase a dream that really can come true;
A silver thread that links the generations,
Evocative of different times and stations.
This game that cast its spell on them as boys
Shall never lose its magic or its joys.
On bumpy village greens or urban swards
The cricketer imagines he's at Lord's.
It's English, it's eccentric, and it's brave;
A living dream we fought two wars to save.

Why do old men love it to the end
And fancy nothing rather than to spend
Their fleeting summers at our cricket grounds
Telling younger men (how sweet that sounds)
Of Compton, Hammond, Graveney and May;
How Trueman blew the Indians away?
Audiences do not dare to doubt them.
Pavilions would not be the same without them.
They find a listening ear despite their age
And feel a part of cricket's heritage.

P.S.
Some ladies love the game without reserve.
It's not, it seems, a gentleman's preserve.
They also play, discreetly, without fuss,
And revel in it's ethos, just like us.
They'll watch alone and never find it boring,
And even volunteer to do the scoring.
Why so? We fella's underestimate
The power that cricket has to fascinate.
They hanker for the feel of bat on ball,
So, men beware. The writing's on the wall!

Printed in Great Britain
by Amazon